By Cyril Aldred

The small shrine from the tomb of Tutankhamun is made in the form of the traditional sanctuary of Nekhebet, the protective goddess of Upper Egypt, who is shown in relief as a vulture flying with outstretched wings across the roof. The Shrine takes the shape of a primitive reed shelter, but is made of wood overlaid with a layer of fine plaster (gesso) and covered with sheets of gold foil worked in low relief with scenes of the king and queen in ceremonies of a religious or semi-religious nature. The front of the shrine is fitted with two doors which are secured by bolts. When the doors are opened, a statuette of King Tutankhamun (illustrated in this book) cast in gold or silver, would have been revealed within; but this was stolen in antiquity by thieves who broke into his tomb. Only the pedestal now remains.

### Back-Panel of a Throne (left)

The back-panel of one of the royal thrones carved in cedar-wood with an openwork design of Heh, the personification of Eternity, wearing a feathered corselet, kneeling on a golden collar, upholding the disk of the sun with its two cobras, symbolizing the King of Upper and Lower Egypt, and supporting three of the names of the king. In the crook of his arm hangs the sign of life; and he holds in each hand a notched palm-rib with a tadpole at its lower extremity on the *shen*-sign, which signifies the entire circuit ruled over by the king as the son of the sun-god. The whole design means that the king rules over his domains for an eternity of years of life. The names of the king are carved in low relief in panels, two of them, left and right, being his Horus name as the earthly representative of the remote sky-god Horus, who is shown as a falcon perched above wearing the crowns of Upper and Lower Egypt. The name of the king in his aspect of Horus is written within a prehistoric palace enclosure and reads: "The Strong Bull  Fair of Births." The other panels show, left, his prenomen, "The King of the North and the South, Lord of the Two Lands, Nebkheperure (Master of Transformations like Re)"; and right, his nomen, "Son of Re, Beloved of Him, Tutankhamun (The Living Image of Amun), Ruler of Thebes, Given Life Forever." On the top rail below the winged disk, emblem of the sun-god Re, is part of a good wish beginning in the centre and reading, right: "Live the Good God, the Image of Re, Protector of the Ruler of Heliopolis, the King Open of Countenance like Thoth . . ." and left: "Live the Good God, the Son of Amun, the Offspring of the Majesty of the Sun-god, Seed of (Re). . ."

### The Roof (next page)

The goddess Nekhebet ("She of the town of Nekheb"—the modern village of El Kab in Upper Egypt) flies across the sky, holding in her talons the *shen*, the symbol of the circuit of the sun over which the king rules: hence his two great names are inscribed in cartouches next to these symbols. The inscription down the centre-line reads:
"The Good God, Lord of the Two Lands,  Neb-kheperu-re , the Son of the Sun-god, of his loins, his beloved, lord of Crowns,  Tut-ankh-amun, Prince of Karnak , Given Life. And the Chief Queen,  Ankhes-en-amun , beloved of Great-of-Magic: may she live!" The name, Neb-kheperu-re, was given to the King at his coronation: his other name, Tut-ankh-aten was bestowed upon him at birth, but the last element was later changed to -amun. Great-of-Magic was a goddess, closely connected with Isis, who was concerned with the crowns of Upper and Lower Egypt, and was usually present therefore at the coronation of the king.

Roof of the little gold shrine of Tut-ankh-amun

The king stands on the left holding his crook and flail sceptres and grasping a lap-wing, symbolizing all the people of Egypt over whom he reigns. He wears a short military wig with streamers at the back. A bull's tail, worn only by pharaohs and certain gods, hangs from the rear of his belt, which also carries a jewelled apron in front tied by a long sash. His wife, Queen Ankhesenamun, stands on the right raising her hands to adore him. She wears a

Left hand door, top panel

similar wig, surmounted by plumes, with a large earring showing beneath it. Her gown also is tied by a long girdle. Both rulers wear the cobra of sovereignty upon the brow. The inscription from top to bottom reads: "The Lord of Upper and Lower Egypt, Nebkheperure (the King's pre-nomen), given life forever. The Lady of the Two Lands, Ankhesenamun, (given life) forever." Below, the king wears the Blue Crown, the so-called war helmet, sewn with roundels, and sits on a cushioned stool with the emblematic plants of Upper and Lower Egypt united between the seat and the stretcher. His feet rest on a hassock. His queen, wearing a gold unguent-container on her head with its cone of perfumed ointment, and a circlet carrying two cobras, offers him bunches of lotus flowers and papyrus rushes, here symbolizing the heraldic plants of Upper and Lower Egypt.

Left hand door, middle panel

The king is wearing a similar costume to that in the top panel. His wife now has her hair confined under a close-fitting cap sewn with roundels and having streamers at the rear. She turns to clasp his arm and lead him into the shrine.

Left hand door, bottom panel

The king now stands on the right wearing a similar costume but with the Blue Crown and holding the crook sceptre only. He raises his right hand to greet the queen, who offers him bunches of lotus flowers and buds. She wears two cobras on her diadem and an elaborate gold unguent-holder on the top of her head containing a cone of perfumed unguent and flanked by two cobras. **The next scene is on the front cover.**

The king sits on a cushioned throne with lion feet and the symbol of the plants of Upper and Lower Egypt united beneath his seat. He wears a striped *nemes* wig-cover with a pigtail at the rear. He holds in his right hand a lotus flower which he has accepted from the bouquet held out to him by the queen, who holds in her right hand the sistrum or rattle used by priest-esses when engaged in the temple services.

Right hand door, top panel

The king wearing the Blue Crown holds both his sceptres in his left hand, while with his right he clasps the hand of the queen opposite, who offers him a bouquet of lotus flowers and buds. She carries an elaborate unguent-holder on top of her short wig which bears a diadem known as the "boatman's circlet," with a bowknot at the back, a cobra at the front and streamers hanging down at the rear and sides.

Right hand door, bottom panel

Both doors have their inner faces decorated with similar panels in relief. This example shows the king standing left, being worshipped by the queen who holds out a sistrum and bouquet to him while a lily flower hangs in the crook of her elbow. Her long wig, with its two lappets falling on her breast as well as a broad mass down her back, is surmounted by a crown with cow-horns, disk and feathers, symbolizing her identity with the great goddess Hathor and the Mistress of Egypt.

Right hand door, inner middle panel

The king wearing the Blue Crown and a long pleated cloak over his royal garb is caressed by his queen who also wears a pleated robe, earrings with pendants and a close-fitting skull-cap sewn with roundels to match his crown.

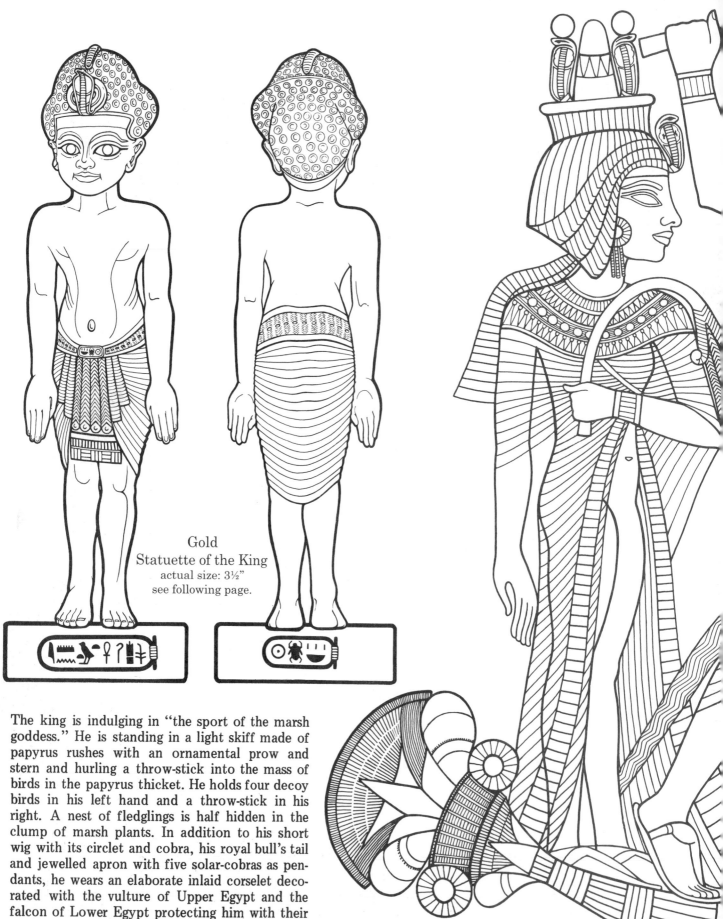

Gold
Statuette of the King
actual size: 3½"
see following page.

The king is indulging in "the sport of the marsh goddess." He is standing in a light skiff made of papyrus rushes with an ornamental prow and stern and hurling a throw-stick into the mass of birds in the papyrus thicket. He holds four decoy birds in his left hand and a throw-stick in his right. A nest of fledglings is half hidden in the clump of marsh plants. In addition to his short wig with its circlet and cobra, his royal bull's tail and jewelled apron with five solar-cobras as pendants, he wears an elaborate inlaid corselet decorated with the vulture of Upper Egypt and the falcon of Lower Egypt protecting him with their wings. Behind him stands his queen wearing a pleated outer robe tied by a long sash, a short military-type wig with unguent-holder, earrings with tasselled pendants and a fly-flapper sceptre.

Left hand side, upper panel, 1st scene

**Tut-ankh-amun's gold dagger** (actual size). When you have colored it gold (cloisonné and wire work on pommel, haft, blade) and red and blue (lily palmettes, falcon with 'eternity symbols, disks, on pommel), you might cut it out and mount it on a stiff cardboard.

**Gold Statuette of the King** (previous page), to color gold and cut out and stand up.

Two staves, one of silver, the other of gold, surmounted by the figure of the king, were found together in a linen wrapping in the tomb of Tutankhamun. Their purpose is unknown, but in view of the fact that the king is shown with the disproportionately large head of an infant, they were probably connected with his coronation rites when he came to the throne as a mere child. He is represented wearing the Blue Crown with its pattern of roundels and the coiled cobra on its front. He wears a pleated kilt secured by a woven belt with a buckle bearing his prenomen, and from which hangs an ornamental jewelled apron. His hands are held in a submissive posture, as though he has just emerged from the shrine where his crown would be placed on his head, and before the crook and flail sceptres have been put into his hands. On the pedestals of these illustrations have been added his prenomen (rear view) and his nomen (front view).

### The Barge of the Gods of Heliopolis

This scene comes from the second of the four shrines that surrounded the great rectangular stone sarcophagus in which King Tutankhamun was laid to rest in his tomb at Western

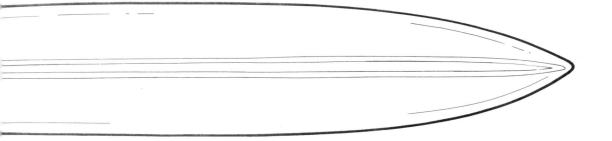

Thebes. The second shrine, like the three others, was made of wood overlaid inside and out with gilded gesso worked in relief with scenes and texts from the sacred books. On the inside of the left hand panel this representation appears of the barge of the different generations of the nine great gods of Heliopolis, the city of the sun-cult in Ancient Egypt. From left to right these are named as: 1. *Re*, the active form of the sun-god, appearing as a falcon-headed man bearing the sun-disk encircled by a cobra upon his vertex. 2. *Atum*, the primordial sun-god who created the universe, shown as a king wearing the Double Crown of Upper and Lower Egypt. 3. *Shu*, the god of the Air who was created by Atum from himself, shown as a man wearing two tall plumes in his long wig. 4. *Tefnut*, the goddess of Moisture, also created by Atum from himself, represented as a woman wearing a close-fitting dress and the long wig of a divinity. 5. *Geb*, the Earth-god, followed by, 6. *Nut*, the sky-goddess, both created by Shu and Tefnut. 7. *Osiris*, the resurrected god, and 8. *Isis*, his wife and sister, both created by Geb and Nut. Lastly, 9. *The King, Lord of the Two Lands, Nebkheperure* (Tutankhamun), the latest manifestation of *Horus* the son of Osiris and Isis. All the male gods wear the long beards of divinities; and with the exception of Osiris and the King they wear corselets of a feather pattern and carry the sign of life in one hand and the sceptre of power in the other.

The king sits on a cushioned fald-stool, his pet lion-cub beside him, while he shoots arrows at birds rising from their nests in the papyrus thickets. He wears a short military wig, gold collars and a pectoral ornament in the form of a winged beetle with sun-disk. A quiver of arrows is slung by a strap over his left shoulder. The goddess Nekhebet in the form of a vulture hovers protectively behind him. At his feet squats his wife on a thick cushion, turning around to hand him an arrow and pointing with her left forefinger at a nest of fledglings, perhaps to warn him against firing at them. She wears a braided side-lock, and a circlet of solar cobras on her short, curled wig.

Left hand side, lower panel

The queen, wearing her crown as the Mistress of Egypt, worships the king with the symbols of the mother goddess Hathor of whom she was chief priestess, *viz.* the sistrum in one hand and the *menyet*-necklace with its counterpoise in the other. The king wears a short military wig and a costume similar to that shown earlier. He carries the crook of authority in his right hand and raises his left in recognition of the worship made by his queen. Above his head is the sun-disk encircled by two cobras, indicating that he is king of Upper and Lower Egypt.

Right hand side, 1st top panel

The king sits on his cushioned throne right, his feet
resting upon a footstool. He wears two necklaces of
disk beads over his floral collar, and a pectoral bearing his names in cartouches hangs on his breast. He
holds out a golden-footed wine cup ornamented with
lotus flowers and leaves within the bowl, but shown
as though they were upright on the rim. His queen,
also wearing similar gold necklaces over her collar,
offers him a bouquet of lotus and poppy flowers and
petals as she pours a choice wine into his cup.

Right hand side, 2nd top panel

The king, right, sits on a cushioned fald-stool covered with a cheetah skin. In his left hand he holds a bouquet of lotus flowers and mandrake fruits (or love-apples). With his right hand he pours perfumed water from a vessel into the cupped hand of his queen, who squats on a cushion at his feet, one elbow resting on his knee, and turns round to look up at him. She wears the sidelock in addition to her short, curled wig, ornamented with the horns, disk, feathers and circlet of solar cobras of a great queen. The whole picture symbolizes the sexual love which the pair bears for each other.

Right hand side, 1st lower panel; all of the scenes on the little gold shrine are here except the 2nd lower panel, which is in TUT-ANKH-AMUN & HIS FRIENDS

The king sits here upon a cushioned throne, wearing the Blue Crown, his feet resting upon a footstool and the protective vulture goddess Nekhebet hovering behind his head holding the signs for life and the expanse of territory over which he rules. His queen leans forward to prepare him for some great ceremony, probably his coronation, by annointing him with an unguent which she holds in the tazza in her other hand, together with a bunch of lotus flowers and buds.

Tut-ankh-amun's *udjat* eye pectoral, worn to help his rebirth.

Rear, upper panel

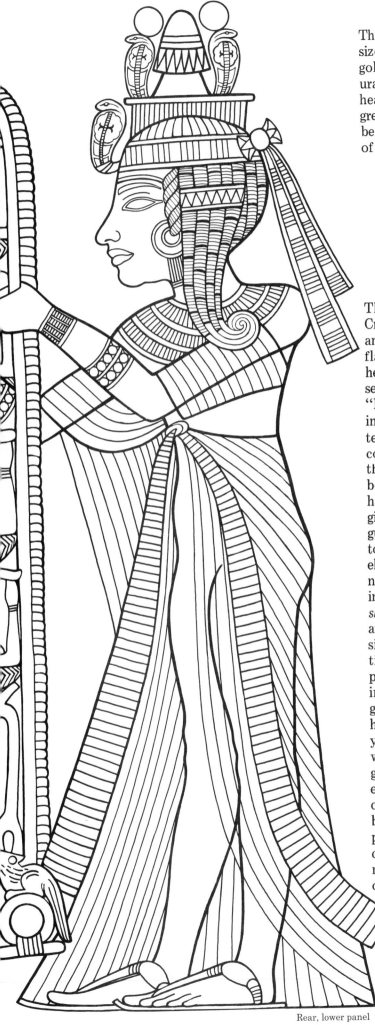

These earrings are actual size; after they are colored gold (disks, frame work, uraei, tails) and blue (birds' heads, feathers) red and green (feathers), they could be cut out, and, with a bit of ingenuity, worn.

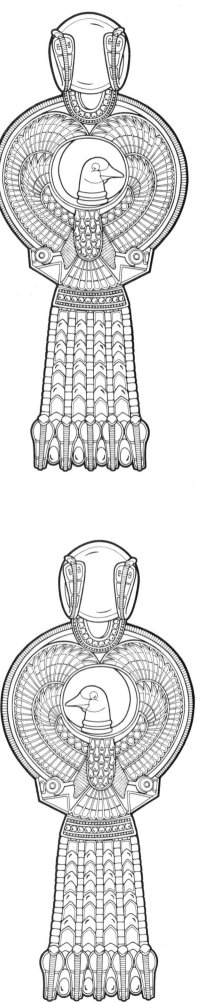

The king, wearing the Red Crown of Lower Egypt, and holding the crook and flail sceptres as "the Shepherd of his People," is seated upon the ancient "Horus throne of the Living" with its feather pattern derived from the falcon god Horus of whom the king is the earthly embodiment. He raises his hand in recognition of the gift which the queen in the guise of a goddess brings to him. This consists of an elaborate device of two notched palm ribs ending in tadpoles resting upon *shen* signs. From them are suspended groups of signs reading, "jubilee festivals" and "all life and power," the whole forming a promise from the gods of a long reign of hundreds of thousands of years of life and power with many jubilees. Such good wishes were usually extended to a king at his coronation or jubilee. Here both scenes on the back panel of the shrine are concerned with the ceremonies of the Coronation of Tutankhamun.

Rear, lower panel

A panel of ivory carved in low relief and stained, from a wooden chest, showing the king seated upon a cushioned throne spread with embroidered cloths, his feet resting upon a cushioned footstool, shooting at fish and pond fowl in a garden pool. He wears a bracer on his left arm to take the rub of the bowstring. His wife, wearing a garlanded unguent cone in a holder on her head, hands him an arrow as she squats on a cushion at his feet. The pool is

shown as a rectangular tank full of fish and water plants. Two birds fly above, one being transfixed by an arrow. Below, a small attendant retrieves a fish and a bird each spitted upon an arrow. The scene is set in an arbor within a garden hung with festoons of flowers and leaves, bouquets of flowers and fruit, interspersed with clumps of mandrakes, poppies and cornflowers. The back cover is taken from the top of the same wooden chest.

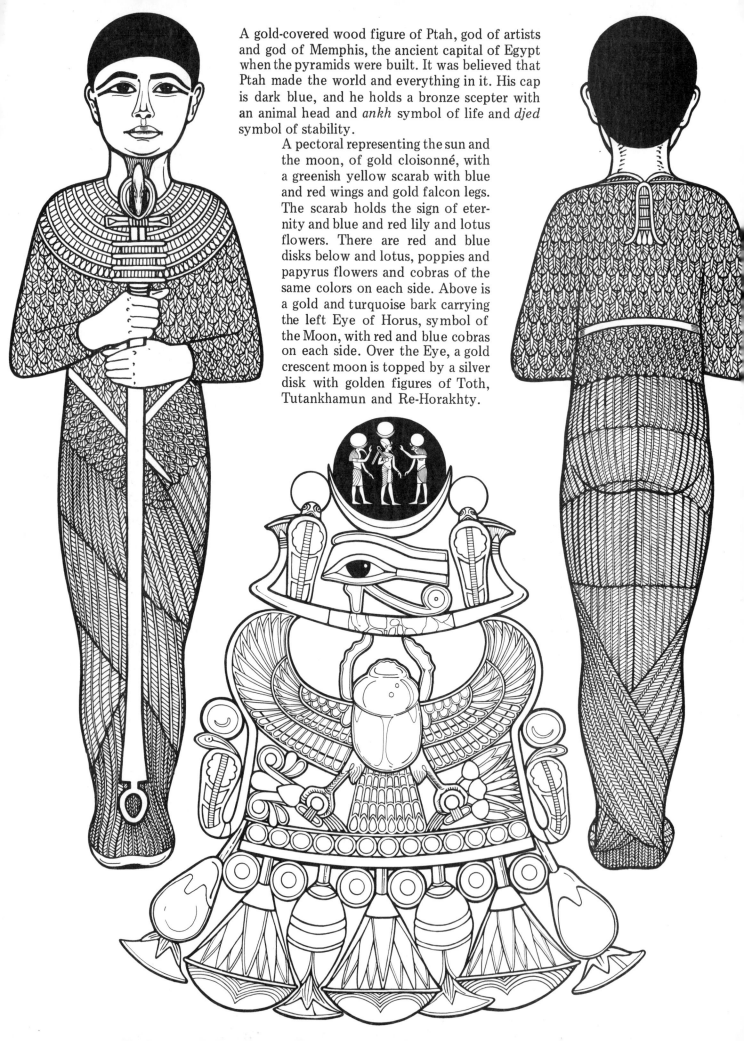

A gold-covered wood figure of Ptah, god of artists and god of Memphis, the ancient capital of Egypt when the pyramids were built. It was believed that Ptah made the world and everything in it. His cap is dark blue, and he holds a bronze scepter with an animal head and *ankh* symbol of life and *djed* symbol of stability.

A pectoral representing the sun and the moon, of gold cloisonné, with a greenish yellow scarab with blue and red wings and gold falcon legs. The scarab holds the sign of eternity and blue and red lily and lotus flowers. There are red and blue disks below and lotus, poppies and papyrus flowers and cobras of the same colors on each side. Above is a gold and turquoise bark carrying the left Eye of Horus, symbol of the Moon, with red and blue cobras on each side. Over the Eye, a gold crescent moon is topped by a silver disk with golden figures of Toth, Tutankhamun and Re-Horakhty.